MILITARY SERVICE

CAREERS IN THE
U.S. MARINE CORPS

MILITARY SERVICE

CAREERS IN THE
U.S. MARINE CORPS

BY EDWARD F. DOLAN

Marshall Cavendish
Benchmark
New York

Special thanks to GySgt Willie C. Cisneros III, assistant Marine officer instructor with the NROTC unit of SUNY Maritime College, Fordham University, and Molloy College in New York, for his review of the manuscript.

MARSHALL CAVENDISH BENCHMARK
99 WHITE PLAINS ROAD
TARRYTOWN, NY 10591
www.marshallcavendish.us

Copyright © 2010 by Marshall Cavendish Corporation

All rights reserved. No part of this book may be reproduced or utilized in any form or by any means electronic or mechanical, including photocopying, recording, or by any information storage and retrieval system, without permission from the copyright holders.

All Internet sites were available and accurate when this book was sent to press.

Library of Congress Cataloging-in-Publication Data

Dolan, Edward F., 1924–
Careers in the U.S. Marine Corps / by Edward F. Dolan.
p. cm. — (Military service)
Includes bibliographical references and index.
Summary: "Discusses service in the U.S. Marine Corps, including training, educational benefits, and career opportunities"—Provided by publisher.
ISBN 978-0-7614-4209-7
1. United States. Marine Corps. 2. United States. Marine Corps—Vocational guidance.
I. Title.
VE23.D648 2008
359.9'602373—dc22
2008039818

EDITOR: Megan Comerford PUBLISHER: Michelle Bisson
ART DIRECTOR: Anahid Hamparian SERIES DESIGNER: Kristen Branch / Michael Nelson Design

Photo research by Candlepants, Incorporated
Cover photo: Dave Fliesen / U.S. Navy Photo

The photographs in this book are used by permission and through the courtesy of: *United States Marine Corps*: Cpl. Rose A. Muth, 7; Sgt. Robert A. Sturkie, 26–27; Cpl. Justin J. Shemanski, 29; Lance Cpl. Chalrie Chavez, 40–41; Sgt. Ryan E. Ohare, 43; Lance Cpl. Carrie Booze, 45; Lance Cpl. Brandon M. Gale, 48; Lance Cpl. Jonathan A. Tabb, 54; Pfc. Peter Zrioka, 63; Lance Cpl. Zachary W. Lester, 64; Cpl. Jess Levens, 66–67; Cpl. Peter R. Miller, 70; Sgt. Jared Hansen, 72. *U.S. Navy Photo*: Photographer 2nd Class Erich J. Ryland, 12–13; Lowell Whitman, 14; Mate 2nd Class Michael Sandberg, 17; Photographer's Mate 2nd Class Daniel J. McLain, 24; Mass Communication Specialist 1st Class Rustum Rivera, 20–21; Gary Nichols, 38–39; Mass Communication Specialist 3rd Class Ja'lon A. Rhinehart, 59. *AP Images*: Laurent Rebours, 2–3; Cpl. Shawn C. Rhodes, 31; Ed Bailey, 32; Ames Tribune, Nirmalendu Majumdar, 35; Julie Jacobson, 56–57; Laura Rauch, 61; Fred Hayes, 10–11, back cover.

Printed in Malaysia
1 3 5 6 4 2

CONTENTS

INTRODUCTION
THE BIRTH OF THE MARINE CORPS 6

ONE
A MARINE'S EQUIPMENT 12

TWO
HOW TO BECOME A MARINE 26

THREE
ENLISTMENT AND TRAINING 40

FOUR
AT WORK AS A MARINE 56

FIVE
SALARY AND BENEFITS 66

ACRONYM GLOSSARY 74

FURTHER INFORMATION 76

INDEX 77

INTRODUCTION

THE BIRTH OF THE MARINE CORPS

The date was November 10, 1775. Just five months earlier the Continental Congress had established an army and, under the command of General George Washington, gone to war with Great Britain in a bid for independence. By mid-October the Congress had called for the creation of a navy. Not long after, on a cold November day, the colonies formed the Continental marines.

Marines, essentially seagoing soldiers, were nothing new on the world stage. Every major seagoing power—from the Roman Empire to Russia, The Netherlands, and Great Britain—had a corps of marines. In sea battles marines had both defensive and offensive roles to fulfill. They protected their ship from enemy forces attempting to board and capture it and they attacked enemy vessels, commandeering the cargoes and subduing the crews. Marines also protected their ship's captain and other officers from an angry or

Thirty-two Marines from the 8th Communications Battalion recite the Oath of Enlistment at Camp Lejeune in North Carolina. The Marine Corps offers different reenlistment incentives, including bonuses and changes in military occupational specialty (MOS).

CAREERS IN THE U.S. MARINE CORPS

mutinous crew. In addition, they guarded their country's shore installations against attacks from sea or land.

The Continental marines initially consisted of two infantry battalions. After the Marines made their first amphibious raid in March 1776, they went on to join the Continental navy in a series of successful coastal raids, and serve alongside the Continental army in the victory at Princeton, New Jersey (1777).

When the Revolutionary War fighting ended in 1781 (the war was not officially over until the Treaty of Paris was signed in 1783), the Continental military forces were disbanded. As settlers spread westward, however, the government decided to maintain a small standing army and established the United States Army.

By the close of the eighteenth century, circumstances had changed. France and Great Britain were both angry at the United States for not taking sides in their renewed hostilities. Both countries began attacking American merchant ships, seizing their cargoes, and taking their crews prisoner. Around the same time American merchant vessels in the Mediterranean Sea fell victim to raiders from the so-called Barbary States of northern Africa.

In response, the Congress of the United States established the U.S. Navy in 1794 and a "Corps of Marines" on July 11, 1798. The corps was to consist of approximately 350 officers and enlisted men who were to act as guards aboard warships, to repel raiders attempting to seize American vessels,

THE BIRTH OF THE MARINE CORPS

and to raid enemy harbors and fortifications. As time passed, the Marines' duties were extended to include the protection of American naval properties—shore batteries, coaling stations, arsenals, and harbors—as well as embassies, consulates, business concerns, and citizens throughout the world. U.S. Marines fought in every major war in which the United States was involved. Though the size of the corps has fluctuated—from no more than 5,000 during the first one hundred years to nearly 800,000 in the Vietnam War—the corps has acted in protection of U.S. rights, properties, and lives worldwide for more than two hundred years.

In the twentieth century the Marine Corps has played a major role in military operations and the global War on Terrorism. Among other things, Marines established a base for operations against the Taliban government in Afghanistan and also headed the invasion force that deposed Iraqi dictator Saddam Hussein.

As of 2009, the Marine Corps consisted of approximately 190,000 officers and enlisted personnel; women accounted for 6.2 percent of personnel. There are an additional 40,000 men and women serving in Marine Corps Reserve units. Today's corps, which is the only self-sustaining force in the U.S. military, is organized into three Marine Expeditionary Forces (MEFs): a naval air force, a ground task force, and three air wings.

This book is aimed primarily at young men and women

CAREERS IN THE U.S. MARINE CORPS

THE BIRTH OF THE MARINE CORPS

Marines Travis Mohler (*left*) and Felix Ramirez check the multi-mode display on the air surveillance radar, which monitored air traffic during the 2002 Winter Olympics. The games, which were held in Salt Lake City, Utah, generated an increase in planes flying to the state.

who are thinking of joining the U.S. Marine Corps. One reader may feel it is his or her patriotic duty. Another might wish to serve to honor the memory of a loved one or friend killed or injured in action. One person may see the Marine Corps as a career. Another may see Marine Corps service as the first step on the road to a university degree or the source of the technical training needed for future civilian work. Still others may join for the oldest reason of all: the desire to meet new people and see faraway places.

Time spent in the Marine Corps, no matter how long, brings rewards. It provides training and a sense of discipline that are useful in civilian life. The academic and practical experience men and women receive in a variety of technical, administrative, and service areas are respected assets in both military and civilian careers. Former members of the military are increasingly sought by civilian employers.

Service with the Marine Corps has quite a lot to offer.

ONE

A MARINE'S EQUIPMENT

MARINES ARE TRAINED IN ELITE BATTLE tactics and survival skills and conduct missions on land, in water, and in the air. Due to the variety and sophistication of these missions, the Marine Corps has an impressive arsenal of equipment—from small weapons to amphibious assault vehicles to helicopters—so it can successfully carry out any operation.

SMALL ARMS

RIFLES, SHOTGUNS, AND HANDGUNS

The Marine Corps uses four kinds of small-arms weapons: rifles and shotguns, handguns, machine guns, and lightweight artillery.

The lightweight, magazine-fed M16A2 service rifle is a Marine's basic weapon. It can be fired from the hip or shoulder from a standing, kneeling,

Japanese soldiers ride in a combat inflatable craft driven by Marine SSgt. David Cleaves, an instructor with the Expeditionary Warfare Training Group Pacific. Cleaves is training the soldiers for amphibious assault operations, water survival, and boat operations.

CAREERS IN THE U.S. MARINE CORPS

or prone position. The rifle can be equipped with an attachment that converts it into an M203 grenade launcher. M16s, along with the launcher attachment, are also standard issue for infantry in the U.S. Army.

The M40A3 sniper rifle is a highly accurate long-range weapon. It is equipped with a special ten-power sniperscope (a magnification lens) that can be changed out for an AN/PVS-10 (Army Navy Passive Viewing System) nightscope. The M40A3, along with the M40A1 that is also used by the Marine Corps, is hand built by corps craftsmen at the Marine Corp Base (MCB) at Quantico, Virginia.

Marines with the 2nd Fleet Antiterrorism Security Team (FAST) fire shotguns as part of weapons familiarization training aboard the USS *Blue Ridge*.

A MARINE'S EQUIPMENT

Marines assigned to guard duty, prisoner supervision, riot control, and other emergency situations carry an 8-pound (3.6 kilogram) 12-gauge shotgun, a repeating weapon that is manually operated by pump action. As of 2009 the Marine Corps was stocking four different makes of 12-gauge shotguns: the Winchester 1200, the Remington 870, and the Mossberg 500 and 590. Some special operations and security forces also use the M1014 joint service combat shotgun.

The semiautomatic M9 Beretta pistol, which Marines can carry in a hip holster for easy access, includes built-in features to prevent accidental discharges. The M9 can be fired as either a single- or double-action weapon. It weighs 2.5 pounds (1.1 kg) when fully loaded with its fifteen-round magazine.

Marines use the reliable and accurate MEU(SOC)— Marine Expeditionary Unit (Special Operations Command)—pistol as a backup weapon when carrying the Heckler and Koch submachine gun. Fully loaded, the MEU weighs 3 pounds (1.4 kg) and, like the M40A1, is hand built.

MACHINE GUNS

The design, weight, accuracy, and reliability of the 9-millimeter MP-5N Heckler and Koch submachine gun have made it the Marine Corps' main weapon for combat in close quarters. It is able to fire in either automatic or semiautomatic modes. It weighs 7.4 pounds (3.4 kg) when loaded with its thirty-round magazine. The handheld M249 light machine gun, known as the squad automatic weapon (SAW) combat machine

CAREERS IN THE U.S. MARINE CORPS

gun, is also widely used in the field. The 16-pound (7.3-kg) SAW comes with a PIP (product improvement program) kit that modifies the barrel, the pistol grip, and the sights.

The Marine Corps also uses three types of vehicle-mounted machine guns: the M240G, the Browning M2, and the MK19 Mod3 grenade machine gun. The 24.2-pound (11-kg) M240G medium machine gun is a 7.62 mm weapon carried aboard tanks and light-armored vehicles to engage enemy infantry, antitank guided-missile teams, and unarmored vehicles. The M2 is a heavy-duty machine gun that fires .50 caliber ammunition and can be mounted on the ground or aboard various vehicles. At 84 pounds (38 kg), it is much heavier than the M240G. The 72.5-pound (33-kg) MK19 Mod3 launches .40 caliber grenades, can be truck mounted, and is used against bunkers, light-armored vehicles, and enemy forces.

LIGHTWEIGHT ARTILLERY

The M224 lightweight mortar is a small cannon that fires 60 mm shells. The barrel, mounted on a bipod that rests on a circular plate, is aimed sharply upward to achieve a high angle of fire. The weapon weighs 46.5 pounds (21 kg).

LARGE EQUIPMENT

ANTIARMOR

The M136 AT4 rocket launcher is a hand-carried 84 mm antiarmor weapon built to stop main battle tanks. Fired from

A MARINE'S EQUIPMENT

U.S. Marines stationed in Kuwait during Operation Enduring Freedom adjust their M198 howitzer field cannon, a medium-range artillery piece.

CAREERS IN THE U.S. MARINE CORPS

the shoulder, this powerful 14.8-pound (6.7-kg) weapon propels a rocket approximately 900 feet (274 meters) in less than one second.

The portable shoulder-launched multipurpose assault weapon (SMAW) is used to destroy main battle tanks, enemy positions, gun emplacements, bunkers, and other obstacles. It fires a high-explosive antiarmor (HEAA) rocket against tanks and a high-explosive dual-purpose (HEDP) rocket against its other targets. The SMAW, which includes a launcher, an electromagnetic firing mechanism, battle sights, and a mount among its equipment, weighs 16.6 pounds (7.5 kg). Both the HEAA and the HEDP rockets are nearly twice as heavy as the launcher itself.

ARMOR

The eight-wheeled light-armored vehicle–mortar (LAV–M) operates in all weather conditions and on all types of terrain. It supports attack and reconnaissance troops with its fire, smoke cover, and nighttime illumination. When fully stocked, the LAV–M carries over ninety-four 81 mm bombs, sixteen rounds of smoke grenades, and eight hundred rounds of 7.62 mm ammunition. It can be transported to a combat area by a cargo plane, but it is also light enough to be carried by the CH-53E helicopter. The Marine Corps uses several models of light-armored vehicles, which are designed for antitank, command-and-control, and logistical functions.

A MARINE'S EQUIPMENT

The Abrams main battle tank (MBT) is the chief combat tank used by the U.S. Army and the Marine Corps. Weighing approximately 61 tons (55.4 kg), the Abrams MBT features armor and a 1,500-horsepower engine. The Abrams's principal armament is a 120 mm smoothbore (unrifled) tank gun, supported by one .50 caliber Browning machine gun and two M240 7.62 mm machine guns. It is manned by a crew of four: a commander, a driver, a gunner, and a loader.

MISSILES

Missiles used by the Marines include the AGM-45 Shrike, an antiradiation missile developed by the Navy to seek out and destroy antiaircraft radars; the AGM-65 Maverick, an air-to-surface radar-guided antitank missile; the AIM-7 Sparrow and the AIM-9 Sidewinder, both air-to-air weapons; and the Hawk, a surface-to-air missile.

AMPHIBIOUS RAID AND RECONNAISSANCE

The combat rubber reconnaissance craft (CRRC) is a lightweight inflatable boat used for reconnaissance, raid, and water missions. The 265-pound (120-kg) CRRC is equipped with a 35-horsepower engine and measures 185 inches (470 centimeters) long, 75 inches (190 cm) wide, and 30 inches (76.2 cm) high. The CRRC was developed to replace all other inflatable boats used by the corps.

CAREERS IN THE U.S. MARINE CORPS

The Marine Corps employs a long list of other raid and reconnaissance equipment including a Marine assault climbers kit (MACK), a parachutist individual equipment kit (PIEK), and an MC-5 static line/free-fall ram air parachute system (SL/FF RAPS).

AIRCRAFT

The Marine Corps uses four main types of aircraft: fighters, transports, helicopters, and rotary-wing aircraft.

FIGHTERS

The AV-8B Harrier is used for combat patrols, armed escort flights, and attack missions against enemy ground-to-air defenses. It takes off vertically, enabling it to depart from sites with limited space, such as ship decks. The Harrier is capable of hovering in midair, so the corps often uses it to provide close-air combat support to ground troops. It fires Maverick

A MARINE'S EQUIPMENT

This MV-22 Osprey takes off after refueling on the amphibious assault ship USS *Nassau*, which was deployed in 2008 to areas in the Atlantic Ocean.

THE LEATHERNECK LEGEND

Ever since the days of the Barbary pirates in the early nineteenth century, Marines have been nicknamed Leathernecks. The moniker is a reference to the uniform worn by U.S. Marines between 1798 and 1872, which featured a 4-inch (10-cm) leather collar.

There is some debate, however, over the purpose of the collar. It was popularly thought to protect the wearer from slashes by an enemy's cutlass, though it has also been suggested that the collar was worn to ensure that a Marine would always hold his head high and proud. Either explanation makes for an interesting tale. The Marine Corps has embraced the name and made it the title of their monthly magazine.

Marines have been known by many other nicknames, including Sea Soldiers, Hard Chargers, Stone Faces, Gyrenes, Devil Dogs, and Jarheads.

According to legend, the nickname *Devil Dogs* was used by World War I German soldiers who were impressed by the fierce tenacity with which the U.S. Marines fought. The name is believed to have originated after five German divisions tried to move through the Belleau Wood to attack Paris, France, in June 1918 and were thwarted by a brigade of U.S. Marines.

Jarheads dates to World War II and seems to be another nickname inspired by the high collar on the Marine dress uniform. The collar was said to make the wearer's head look as if it were sticking out of the mouth of a mason jar. The name was coined by sailors who expected the epithet to generate anger. Instead, the Marines liked it and took it as a sign of respect.

A MARINE'S EQUIPMENT

and Sidewinder missiles, as well as other ammunitions. As of 2009, there were 175 Harriers in service.

The Marine Corps also flies the F/A-18 Hornet, which is equipped with precision-guided missiles, bombs, a nose cannon, and sophisticated computer systems. These fighters engage in air-to-air and air-to-ground combat.

TRANSPORT

A combination transport and tanker, the KC-130 Hercules, which is used by both the Marine Corps and the Air Force, is one of the military's most versatile aircraft. The Hercules transports combat troops or cargo. It also provides in-flight fueling for planes and helicopters; two fueling pods enable it to simultaneously transfer approximately three hundred gallons (1,136 liters) per minute to two aircraft. In addition, the Hercules handles weather reconnaissance flights, aeromedical evacuations, and disaster-relief missions. In 2009 there were seventy-five KC-130s in service in the Marine Corps and the Reserve.

HELICOPTERS

The UH-1Y Huey is one of the most technologically advanced helicopters available. As an airlift utility helicopter, it is flown in combat-assault and search-and-rescue missions, used to evacuate the wounded, and provides fire support to troops in combat. The Marine Corps boasts that the UH-1Y can

CAREERS IN THE U.S. MARINE CORPS

A UH-1N Huey helicopter hovers in the air as Marines rappel to the ground in a Marine Air-Ground Task Force (MAGTF) demonstration of air and ground attacks used by the Marine Corps.

A MARINE'S EQUIPMENT

support any mission. It even has night-vision-goggle–compatible cockpits for crews flying missions at night.

The MV-22 Osprey, the world's first tilt-rotor aircraft, has vertical takeoff and landing (VTOL) capabilities. Once airborne, it can be converted to a turboprop airplane for high-speed, high-altitude flight. The U.S. Air Force also has a version—the CV-22 Osprey. As of early 2009, the V-22s were still under development and only being used in special operations missions. Neither the Marine Corps nor the Air Force had fully assimilated the Osprey into its air fleet. The Osprey will be used for the secret insertion of troops into enemy territory at night, supply deliveries, and troop removal. The Marine Corps intends to replace the CH-46E Sea Knight and CH-53D Sea Stallion helicopters, both of which currently provide assault support, with 360 Ospreys.

HOW TO BECOME A MARINE

THERE ARE FOUR WAYS TO SERVE IN THE U.S. Marine Corps: by enlisting in the active-duty Marine Corps, joining the Marine Corps Reserve or the Naval Reserve Officers Training Corps (NROTC) program, or graduating from the U.S. Naval Academy at Annapolis, Maryland. Naval academy graduates and those who complete NROTC programs enter the Marine Corps as second lieutenants; they can also join the Navy as ensigns. All men and women interested in becoming U.S. Marines must meet certain requirements.

- They must be a U.S. citizen or meet noncitizen requirements.
- They must be between the ages of seventeen and thirty-four; those who are seventeen need parental consent.

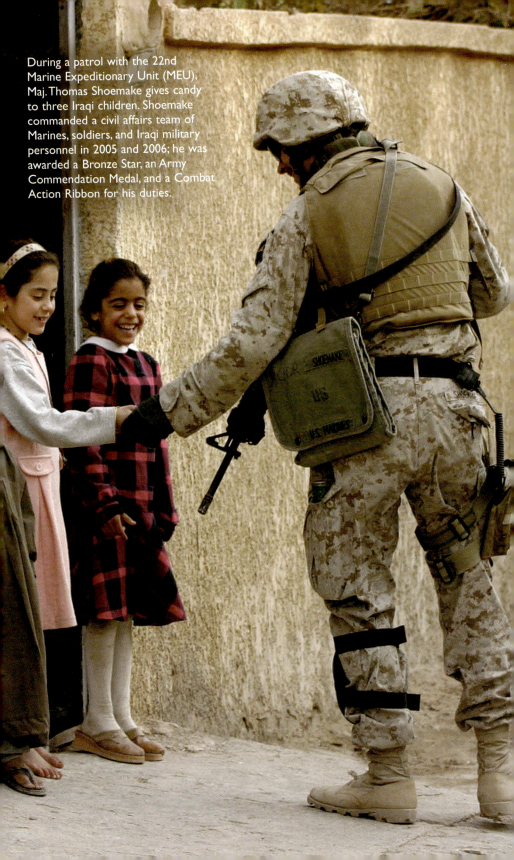

During a patrol with the 22nd Marine Expeditionary Unit (MEU), Maj. Thomas Shoemake gives candy to three Iraqi children. Shoemake commanded a civil affairs team of Marines, soldiers, and Iraqi military personnel in 2005 and 2006; he was awarded a Bronze Star, an Army Commendation Medal, and a Combat Action Ribbon for his duties.

CAREERS IN THE U.S. MARINE CORPS

- They must be high school graduates or have a high school equivalency diploma.

Enlistees must also pass urinalysis tests for drug and alcohol abuse and meet a variety of legal and medical standards.

The Marine Corps also has physical standards for enlistment. Men and women must pass the corps' initial strength test (IST) and the physical fitness test (PFT). Those who fail are assigned to the Physical Conditioning Platoon and remain there until they pass the IST and PFT. A recruiting officer will advise enlistees to undertake an exercise and diet program prior to beginning their recruit training.

ON ACTIVE DUTY WITH THE MARINE CORPS

First-time Marine Corps enlistees sign on for a four- to six-year tour of duty. At the end of the initial enlistment period—or any subsequent one—a Marine may return to civilian life or reenlist. As of 2009, there were 190,000 men and women on active duty as Marines.

Life in the Marine Corps begins with boot camp (known as basic combat training in the Army and basic military training in the Air Force), a thirteen-week period of military training. Men and women who successfully complete boot camp continue on to a period of schooling or on-the-job training in one of the corps' job fields.

HOW TO BECOME A MARINE

Receiving Drill Instructor SSgt. Kendall Jones stands with new recruits in front of the silver hatches at the Recruit Processing Center. Once they have entered the center, recruits will finalize paperwork and get haircuts. They turn in all civilian clothing and belongings and are issued their first Marine Corps uniforms.

MARINE CORPS RESERVE

Service with the U.S. Marine Corps Reserve (USMCR) offers several options for men and women who wish to serve; he or she can serve part-time with an active-duty unit, full time with a Reserve unit close to home, or on a special task force for no longer than 179 days. The Reserve's motto is "Ready, Willing, Able," which reflects the loyalty and preparedness emphasized by the Marine Corps.

CAREERS IN THE U.S. MARINE CORPS

As with the Reserve programs of the other military branches, USMCR duty generally entails a commitment to monthly weekend drills and participation in an annual two-week training period. This traditional form of reserve duty is offered by the Selected Marine Corps Reserve (SMCR); most service is done as a unit. The USMCR also provides the broadest range of training opportunities in military occupational specialties (MOSs) (many of the other forms of USMCR duty are based on previously acquired training).

The Marine Forces Reserve (MARFORRES) is the reserve program for the Marine Corps, headquartered in New Orleans, Louisiana. It includes both the reservists and the active-duty Marines that keep the Reserve forces combat ready. MARFORRES augments and reinforces active forces by training and providing units and individual Marines for crisis situations that require extra support.

The Active Reserve (AR) is one of the special programs offered by the USMCR. Marines coming off active duty who want to remain close to home but still serve in the corps often opt to serve as full-time recruiters, administrators, or instructors with the AR.

The Individual Mobilization Augmentees (IMA) program is geared toward reservists with a specialized skill who can fulfill a need of an active-duty unit. The IMA program is the most flexible, since service depends on the reservist's ability and the active-duty demand for that ability.

HOW TO BECOME A MARINE

Lt. Gen. Dennis M. McCarthy, commanding general, Marine Forces Reserve, visits Task Force Tarawa at Blair Airfield, Iraq, on May 1, 2003. During the visit he spoke with Marines of Reserve unit 3rd Battalion, 23rd Marine Regiment.

USMCR also offers an Active Duty Special Work (ADSW) service option in which Reserve Marines fulfill a need of the active-duty corps. ADSW tours last less than six months and provide support for a range of USMC activities.

Marines who sign up for the Individual Ready Reserve (IRR) often have some time remaining on their active-duty or Reserve contracts, but have fulfilled their requirements. IRR members must meet physical and uniform requirements once a year.

WOMEN IN THE MARINE CORPS

Women have been allowed to serve as full-fledged U.S. Marines since 1948. Prior to that year they were limited to service as nurses and office personnel in times of war. They account for about 6 percent of today's Marine Corps personnel, the lowest percentage of the military branches.

Despite their relatively recent official acceptance into the U.S. armed forces, women have been serving with the country's military since the Revolutionary War. One of the most recognizable names from the colonial era is Molly Pitcher (her real name was Mary Ludwig

Hays), who carried water to troops in the 1778 Battle of Monmouth. During the Civil War women served as nurses, though some disguised themselves as men and fought.

Approximately 34,000 women served during World War I, more than 300 of which volunteered with the Marine Corps, performing clerical duties. In World War II the number of women volunteering with the Marine Corps jumped to more than 23,000, though most still worked in administrative fields; women were allowed to officially enlist with the corps following the war.

By the end of the war, the work of the approximately 350,000 women serving with the armed forces had won them recognition. In 1948 they gained a permanent place in the nation's military forces with the passage of the Women's Armed Services Integration Act. The measure codified the position of women in the military. Like men, they could hold regular military rank and enjoy the privileges that came with rank. Limitations were placed on enlistment and promotion, however, and they were barred from combat duty.

Since then, the role of women in the military has grown steadily. Between 1,000 and 3,000 female Marines served in the Korean, Vietnam, and Gulf wars. A number of court rulings enabled female officers to command units composed of both men and women and ended the separate training of men and women. Court decisions also made the financial entitlements for dependents equal for both men and women in the service.

In addition, opportunities that had once been limited to men were extended to women. In the 1970s the first female students were admitted to the U.S. Naval Academy at Annapolis, the Military Academy at West Point, and the Air Force Academy in Colorado Springs. Women are now free to hold any job in the Marine Corps except for those that require placement in combat areas.

Left: Two lines of young women in the Marine Corps' Delayed Entry Program stand at attention as Marine SSgt. Tama Richardson instructs them. The women, who are all from the five boroughs of New York City, will eventually report for recruit training at MCD Parris Island.

CAREERS IN THE U.S. MARINE CORPS

Associate duty is a good option for Marines who have completed their active-duty contracts and would like to continue service as a reservist, but are focusing on adjusting to civilian life. They can drill with a Reserve unit, thus maintaining their readiness as a Marine, without formally joining the unit (or getting paid). When he or she is ready, the transition to USMCR duty is easy.

All reservists can be called to active duty—such as in times of war or during a national emergency—at which point they are paid the equivalent of an active-duty Marine at the same rank. Federal law limits a reservist's service period to two years. Under most circumstances the law also requires the reservist's civilian employer to give a returning reservist his or her former job. The reservist must have notified his or her employer of the call to duty and must return immediately to work. As of early 2009 there were approximately 40,000 men and women on Reserve duty, not including the nearly 60,000 Marines in the IRR.

NAVAL RESERVE OFFICERS TRAINING CORPS

The Naval Reserve Officers Training Corps (NROTC) was founded in 1926, sixty-four years after Congress established the ROTC program for the U.S. Army. The Marine Corps joined the NROTC program shortly thereafter, in 1932. The U.S. Air Force also sponsors a ROTC program.

HOW TO BECOME A MARINE

All ROTC programs depend upon the cooperation of participating universities and colleges. Since the 1990s, the number of ROTC programs has increased to produce approximately 60 percent of all military officers. As of 2009, colleges and universities in thirty-four states and the District of Columbia offered NROTC programs.

In 1972 the Secretary of the Navy authorized sixteen women to enroll in the NROTC program. In 1990 the pro-

Twenty-eight cadets with the NROTC program at Iowa State University march in formation for a ceremony in their honor in 2004.

CAREERS IN THE U.S. MARINE CORPS

gram was expanded to include students participating in a four-year nursing course; the graduates are granted commissions in the Navy Nurse Corps. The Marine Corps does not have its own nursing corps; it is cared for by Navy personnel.

The essentials of NROTC programs are much the same on all campuses. The program has three basic requirements: to wear the NROTC uniform once a week, to participate in unit lectures, drill instruction, and inspection at least once a week, and to attend a naval science course each semester. In every other aspect, the campus life of an NROTC student is no different from that of his or her fellow students.

An NROTC cadet must complete a regular college course load for a bachelor's degree; studies must include calculus, calculus-based physics, English grammar and composition, and a course in national security policy or American military affairs.

The NROTC program offers scholarships to assist students. The scholarships, which are based on merit and not need, provide full tuition, funds for textbooks and uniforms, and a stipend.

A cadet is commissioned after completing his or her NROTC studies. The new officer is obligated to complete eight years of military service—four years on active duty and four years on Reserve duty—after which he or she may make a career as an officer with the U.S. Navy or the Marine Corps, or become a member of the Reserve.

HOW TO BECOME A MARINE

U.S. NAVAL ACADEMY

The U.S. Naval Academy (USNA) in Annapolis, Maryland, was founded in 1845 by the Secretary of the Navy as the Naval School. It opened its doors on October 10, staffed with seven male professors, to fifty male students. Prior to its founding, young officers had been trained aboard their ships by teachers and fellow officers.

The school was renamed the U.S. Naval Academy in 1850. Students were called cadets until 1902, when the name was changed to midshipmen. Midshipmen are officer cadets. Women were first admitted in 1976 and make up more than 20 percent of the academy's 2011 graduating class. About 4,600 men and women enroll in the Naval Academy each year.

The academy trains officers for both the Navy and the Marine Corps. All USNA students complete four years of study in mathematics, science, engineering, the social sciences, and the humanities, and are awarded bachelor of science (BS) degrees. Graduates joining the Marine Corps are commissioned as second lieutenants; those bound for the Navy are commissioned as ensigns.

Admittance to the Naval Academy is competitive and prospective students need a nomination to be considered for entrance. Applicants must submit letters requesting a nomination to the vice president of the United States, the Secretary of the Navy, or a member of Congress. Like any

CAREERS IN THE U.S. MARINE CORPS

HOW TO BECOME A MARINE

2007 Graduates of Officer Candidate School in Pensacola, Florida, are commissioned during a ceremony at the National Museum of Naval Aviation.

other university, the Naval Academy also requires an application, a personal statement, and letters of recommendation.

The government provides money for the student's tuition, supplies, and board, and pays him or her a salary equivalent to that of an ensign. After graduation, the new officer must serve on active duty for at least five years.

THREE

ENLISTMENT AND TRAINING

ANY DECISION THAT WILL INVOLVE FOUR or more years of a person's life is an important one. The decision to join the Marine Corps is no exception. It can be helpful to talk with family, friends, and even a favorite teacher before making a final decision. Whatever the motivation for joining, the first step is enlisting.

ENLISTMENT

Enlistment begins at a local Marine Corps recruiting station, where a recruiter will provide an introduction to life in the Marine Corps and answer a prospective enlistee's questions. Once the final decision is made, the enlistee needs to bring a number of documents to the recruiter for review:

1. Birth certificate
2. Social Security card

Marine Corps recruits finish the final—and longest—hike of the Crucible, the last challenge of boot camp.

CAREERS IN THE U.S. MARINE CORPS

3. High school diploma and, if applicable, college transcript
4. A list of jobs held and places worked since age sixteen
5. Contact information for four personal references
6. A list of problems with the police, if any, including minor traffic violations
7. A list of places visited outside the United States
8. A list of places lived since age sixteen
9. A medical history, including a list of current medications

Noncitizens need to bring their permanent resident (green card) number and port of entry place and date.

After this information has been reviewed and discussed with the enlistee, the recruiter will fill out a preliminary medical report that will be reviewed by a doctor. Once cleared, the enlistee is sent to a local military entrance processing station (MEPS), where he or she undergoes a complete physical examination (including hearing and vision testing, blood and urinalysis, and a pregnancy test for women) and takes the Armed Services Vocational Aptitude Battery (ASVAB).

The ASVAB consists of a series of multiple-choice tests. It is not an intelligence (IQ) or academic test; its main purpose is to target the career best suited for the enlistee based on his or her interests and abilities. The ASVAB tests aptitude in several areas: general science, arithmetic reasoning, electronics, and mechanical comprehension.

After the medical examination and the vocational testing are complete, the enlistee interviews with a career classifier, who will advise the enlistee on career possibilities and

ENLISTMENT AND TRAINING

CWO3 Lauren LaVine swore in his two daughters, Shannon and Nicole, at the Naval Station at Pearl Harbor. The two young women are continuing a family tradition: their grandfather and great-grandfather were also Marines.

review his or her background. Finally, with a counselor present, the enlistee will review and sign the enlistment contract.

Upon completion of these steps comes the oath of enlistment ceremony. Enlistees stand before a commissioned officer and recite the oath that makes them members of the U.S. Marine Corps:

> I, _____, do solemnly swear (or affirm) that I will support and defend the Constitution of the United States against all enemies, foreign and domestic; that I will bear true faith and allegiance to the same; and that I will obey the orders of the President of the United States and the orders

CAREERS IN THE U.S. MARINE CORPS

of the officers appointed over me, according to regulations and the Uniform Code of Military Justice.

Not everyone who has taken the oath of enlistment proceeds immediately to boot camp; some take advantage of the Marine Corps' Delayed Entry Program (DEP), which allows an enlistee to wait as long as a year before reporting for duty. After the enlistment ceremony, people in the program return to school, work, or family, business, or personal matters. Even though their lives as civilians continue, they are still in the Marine Corps and must report for duty at the agreed-upon time.

BOOT CAMP

New enlistees must report to a recruit depot for thirteen weeks of basic military instruction referred to as recruit training or boot camp. Marine Corps boot camp is the most challenging, both physically and mentally, of all the military basic training programs. There are written exams, practical application tests, and inspections throughout boot camp.

The Marine Corps maintains two facilities for boot camp. Male recruits living east of the Mississippi River and all female recruits are sent to the Marine Corps Recruit Depot (MCRD) Parris Island in South Carolina, which trains approximately 17,000 Marines every year; the men and women train together but are housed in separate quarters. The MCRD in San Diego, California, is the training center for

ENLISTMENT AND TRAINING

Pvt. Mahomad Luckett struggles to pull himself over the final log in the Dirty Name obstacle, part of boot camp at MCRD San Diego.

male recruits who live west of the Mississippi. Approximately 21,000 recruits train at MCRD San Diego annually.

Physical training is a major component of boot camp for a recruit and continues to be important throughout a Marine's entire military career. The Marine Corps runs its

CAREERS IN THE U.S. MARINE CORPS

own physical fitness program aimed at keeping Marines in peak performance shape to ensure that they can handle the challenges of any operational environment.

Throughout boot camp, chaplains and training officers, as well as drill instructors, emphasize the USMC core values: honor, courage, and commitment. These three values, which are considered the basis of every Marine's character, are also expected to serve as the foundation for other values important to a recruit's success as a Marine.

MARINE CORPS TRAINING MATRIX

Recruit training is divided into three phases: basic learning, rifle training, and field training. Both physical and classroom training is incorporated into all three phases. Before recruit training officially begins, uniforms, footwear, and toiletries are distributed, and all males' heads are shaved during recruit "receiving." Physical and dental screenings and a strength test—pull-ups, sit-ups, and a 1.5-mile (2.4-km) run—are also completed at this time.

The first part of week one is called "forming." Recruits are assigned to a training company and introduced to drill instructors (DI) who "form" new recruits into Marines. DIs teach recruits the basics of military conduct and protocol—how to wear their Marine Corps uniforms, march, salute properly, address their superiors, and secure their weapons.

Unlike the Army, Navy, and Air Force, where enlistees enter training at the most basic rank, an enlistee at Marine

ENLISTMENT AND TRAINING

Corps boot camp is simply called "recruit" until he or she demonstrates the military skills, self-discipline, leadership, and motivation required of a U.S. Marine.

PHASE 1: BASIC LEARNING

The first twenty-four days of recruit training are structured to establish and reinforce the core values—honor, courage, and commitment—and ethics. Part of the first phase is combat conditioning, which entails physical training in self-defense, bayonet and knife techniques, pugil sticks, rappelling, gas-mask drills, and other such exercises. Recruits also receive basic instruction in the Marine Corps Martial Arts Program (MCMAP), which trains Marines to act on instinct and become proficient in hand-to-hand combat.

During phase one, courses are taught in core value training, Marine Corps history, equal opportunity, and sexual harassment. Recruits also learn first aid, go on conditioning marches, and compete in obstacle courses. Near the end of phase one recruits must pass the combat water survival (CWS) exercise; all recruits must pass CWS level four before continuing on to the next phase of boot camp.

PHASE 2: RIFLE TRAINING

Recruits generally learn the fundamentals of marksmanship in the fifth week of boot camp. They are coached in the techniques of handling the Marine Corps' basic weapon: the M16A2 service rifle. Recruits learn the four basic firing posi-

CAREERS IN THE U.S. MARINE CORPS

tions—standing, sitting, kneeling, and prone—and are instructed in the correct sighting and firing techniques, including how to adjust to weather conditions. Additional training includes coaching in weapons handling in various field situations; recruits fire in adverse light, at moving targets, at multiple targets, and while wearing a gas mask.

The second phase also includes longer conditioning marches, a PFT, obstacle courses, and classroom instruction. Combat conditioning and core value training continues, as well.

Sgt. John A. Wallace, a combat instructor with the Marine Combat Training Battalion, explains the fundamentals of patrol duty to a group of new Marines.

ENLISTMENT AND TRAINING

PHASE 3: FIELD TRAINING

The evaluation process begins during the third phase of boot camp. Recruits continue their training in marksmanship, combat conditioning, and the Marine Corps's core values. Basic Warrior Training (BWT) also begins during phase three, which introduces recruits to field living conditions and basic field skills, such as how to pitch a tent and how to maintain sanitary conditions.

Recruits must sit for classes in sexual assault and the educational benefits offered by the military, as well as successfully complete a final PFT administered a week before graduation.

THE CRUCIBLE The Crucible is a fifty-four-hour exercise designed to make recruits apply all they have learned during training to a simulated battlefield situation. It is a challenging and exhausting climax to boot camp. Teams of recruits face a series of intense mental and physical combat challenges, including marches, patrols with squads and fire teams, land navigation problems, rationing a limited amount of food, and running the four warrior stations.

Each warrior station is a course that features several activities presenting a string of problems that each team must solve within four hours. For example, one station may call for a team to cross an enemy rope bridge that has been rigged with explosives. Equipped with only two short ropes, personal gear, and their wits, the teammates must devise a way of getting safely across the bridge. Another event may require the team to fire

CAREERS IN THE U.S. MARINE CORPS

its way through a series of pop-up targets, or teams may have to battle each other with pugil sticks.

Teams go through a 5-mile (8-km) night march, a night assault course, and the 9-mile (14.5-km) march that ends the Crucible. Recruits march 42 miles (67.6 km) during the entire event.

GRADUATION The Crucible comes to a close with a march at dawn that ends at the replica of the Marine Corps Memorial (known as the Iwo Jima Memorial) on the base's parade ground. There, a color guard raises the flag, a chaplain reads a prayer, and the company's first sergeant gives a speech congratulating the recruits on successfully completing the Crucible and boot camp. At the graduation ceremony, drill instructors present each recruit with the Marine Corps insignia—the eagle, globe, and anchor. The instructor shakes each recruit's hand and for the first time addresses each one as "Marine."

ON-DUTY TRAINING

After completing boot camp the new Marines report to either the Infantry Training Battalion (ITB) or the Marine Combat Training Battalion (MCT Bn). ITB prepares new Marines for the infantry MOS over the course of fifty-two days while the twenty-nine-day MCT Bn trains non-infantry Marines in basic combat skills. Upon the completion of either ITB or MCT Bn, a Marine is assigned to a base for instruction in his or her career specialty.

ENLISTMENT AND TRAINING

ENLISTED RANKS

Few things in the life of a Marine have more daily impact than rank, and rank is directly linked to pay. A rank is a title, and a pay grade is an alphanumeric designation. All members of the U.S. military fall within three categories of rank: enlisted personnel, warrant officers, and commissioned officers. All pay grades for enlisted personnel begin with the letter E.

The lowest Marine Corps enlisted ranks are that of Private (E-1), Private First Class (E-2), and Lance Corporal (E-3). Marines in these ranks do not have leadership responsibilities; they are expected to perform all assigned tasks.

The ranks of Corporal (E-4) and Sergeant (E-5) are noncommissioned officer (NCO) ranks. NCOs are enlisted Marines who have shown themselves to have command capabilities. A commissioned officer usually has at least a college degree and has undergone special training; he or she delegates responsibility to all NCOs. Corporals and sergeants are expected to supervise and guide junior Marines.

Staff Sergeant (E-6), Gunnery Sergeant (E-7), Master Sergeant (E-8), First Sergeant (E-8), Master Gunnery Sergeant (E-9), and Sergeant Major (E-9) are staff noncommissioned officer (SNCO) ranks. SNCOs are responsible for the supervision of subranking personnel and for acting as advisers to their commanding officers on all matters pertaining to enlisted personnel.

The rank of Sergeant Major of the Marine Corps (E-9) is the corps' highest enlisted rank. Unlike the other SNCO

MARINE CORPS RANK INSIGNIA

ENLISTED RANKS

All Marines wear the Marine Corps insignia—an eagle perched atop a globe with an anchor through it—in addition to their rank insignia.

Private (Pvt): no rank insignia

 Private First Class (PFC)

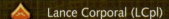 Lance Corporal (LCpl)

Corporal (Cpl)

Sergeant (Sgt)

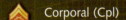 Staff Sergeant (SSgt)

Gunnery Sergeant (GySgt)

 Master Sergeant (MSgt)

First Sergeant (1stSgt)

 Master Gunnery Sergeant (MGySgt)

Sergeant Major (SgtMaj)

Sergeant Major of the Marine Corps (SgtMajMC)

OFFICERS

Gold and silver bars, leaves, stars, and even an eagle are used in the rank insignia worn by officers in the Marine Corps.

Second Lieutenant (2LT)

First Lieutenant (1LT)

Captain (CPT)

Major (MAJ)

Lieutenant Colonel (LTC)

Colonel (COL)

Brigadier General (BG)

Major General (MG)

Lieutenant General (LTG)

General (GEN)

WARRANT OFFICERS

Warrant Officer (WO)

Chief Warrant Officer (CWO2)

Chief Warrant Officer (CWO3)

Chief Warrant Officer (CWO4)

Chief Warrant Officer (CWO5)

CAREERS IN THE U.S. MARINE CORPS

A student in Marine Combat Training practices loading and unloading a mounted machine gun before firing the weapon.

ranks, only one person can be the Sergeant Major of the Marine Corps. He or she assists and advises the corps commandant, a commissioned officer.

MARINE CORPS OFFICERS

Most Marines earn officer commissions by graduating from the NROTC program or the Naval Academy, or by completing either the Platoon Leader Course (PLC) or the Officer Candidates Course (OCC) offered at the Officer Candidates School (OCS) in Quantico, Virginia.

ENLISTMENT AND TRAINING

The PLC produces 35 percent of all Marine Corps officers—the largest percentage of all commissioning options. Over the course of two six-week sessions, college freshmen and sophomores undergo physical, academic, and leadership courses. College juniors can also take the PLC, however they attend a ten-week training session. College seniors or graduates interested in being a Marine Corps officer attend the ten-week OCC. Both the PLC and OCC test that candidates are physically and mentally qualified to be officers; OCS students must also prove that they embody honor, courage, and commitment, the Marine Corps core values. After receiving a commission as a second lieutenant, new officers must attend The Basic School (TBS) and specialize in ground, aviation, or law. At TBS men and women are assigned an MOS and begin training.

Commissioned Marine Corps officers are classified into nine pay grades, designated by the letter O, and ten ranks. Officers in pay grades O-1 to O-3 are company grade officers, those in grades O-4 to O-6 are field grade officers, and those in O-7 and higher are called general officers. Commissioned officers hold presidential appointments that are confirmed by the Senate.

Warrant officers are highly trained experts in a specific field. They are given warrants from the Marine Corps service secretary and receive presidential commissions upon promotion to chief warrant officer 2. The five pay grades are designated by the letter W.

FOUR

AT WORK AS A MARINE

U.S. MARINES ARE FIRST AND FOREMOST thoroughly trained soldiers who serve whenever and wherever they are needed. Every Marine also works in a specific field of his or her choosing. The many jobs offered help the Marine Corps meet daily responsibilities.

The jobs that are open to enlisted Marines are known as military occupational specialties (MOS); no degree is required. As any U.S. Marine will tell a new enlistee, "A Marine is what you are. Your MOS is the job you do."

MILITARY OCCUPATIONAL SPECIALTIES

The Marine Corps divides its MOSs into groups called occupational fields (OccFld). An OccFld

LCpl. Ana Taras of Brooklyn, New York, is the only female mechanic working on the flight line in her Marine Corps helicopter squadron. Here she is servicing the engine of a CH-53E Super Sea Stallion.

MOS DESIGNATION

The Marine Corps uses a four-digit designation to identify all MOSs. The OccFlds are numbered 01 through 99. The OccFld is represented in the first two digits of the MOS. The second two MOS digits indicate the Marine's actual job title, such as light-armored vehicle crewman.

For example, MOS 0369 indicates that the Marine serves in OccFld 03, Infantry, as an infantry unit leader. MOS 0911 designates OccFld 09, Training, and the drill instructor MOS. Each of the specific jobs—MOSs—is associated with certain ranks; a private cannot be an infantry unit leader, and a master gunnery sergeant will not be a rifleman.

usually consists of a grouping of jobs with similar functions; there are fields in intelligence, communications, infantry, engineering, and construction. OccFlds may contain many jobs or only one, and each job within a field has different personnel requirements. Fields 85 through 90 are classified as category B occupational specialties and consist of temporary assignments that are performed by Marines who also have a full-time MOS.

INFANTRY

OccFld 03, Infantry, incorporates the basic positions required for a combat unit: rifleman, machine gunner, mortarman, assaultman, light-armored vehicle crewman, anti-tank assault guided missileman, and infantry unit leader. Since U.S. military policy prohibits assigning women to combat duties, Infantry is open to men only.

AT WORK AS A MARINE

Marines from the 9th Engineer Support Battalion assemble a bridge during a joint training exercise with Navy Seabees in Japan in 2006. Since Marine engineers and Navy Seabees may be stationed in the same area, it is important that the units be able to work together.

CAREERS IN THE U.S. MARINE CORPS

Each OccFld 03 position requires broad training. Basic tactical training (both offensive and defensive), battlefield survival techniques, decision making, and combat first aid are all part of Infantry training. A rifleman, for example, will also be trained as a scout, a sniper, a reconnaissance soldier, an assault team member, and an expert in close combat; he will also learn how to handle the basic hand weapons of the Marine Corps.

PERSONNEL AND ADMINISTRATION

Marines working in OccFld 01, Personnel and Administration, attend to the corps' administrative and clerical duties, including those related to its personnel and its postal system. All Marines working in this field are trained in one or more office and administrative skills: office management, computer operation, correspondence, record keeping and filing, postal operations, and personnel management.

INTELLIGENCE

Personnel working in Intelligence (OccFld 02) are responsible for the collection, processing, and dissemination of intelligence information, such as enemy positions and strategies. Marines in this field are required to attend and pass formal schooling, must master analytical and technical skills, and may specialize in counterintelligence, technical surveillance countermeasures, geographic intelligence, or imagery analysis.

AT WORK AS A MARINE

Many Marine Corps units have been deployed to the Middle East in the twenty-first century. Members of the 3rd Battalion engage Iraqi soldiers and provide cover for Sgt. Jesse Lanter as he carries injured Cpl. Barry Lange off the battlefield in 2003. In boot camp Marines begin preparing for battlefield situations.

TRAINING

OccFld 09, Training, is essential to the Marine Corps's reputation as one of the best-trained military forces in the world. There are several MOSs in this field, including drill instructor, Marine combat instructor, martial arts instructor, water safety/survival instructor, and marksmanship instructor. Most men and women in OccFld 09 train predominantly entry-level Marines, though some, such as martial arts instructors, also train Marines assigned to operating forces that necessitate specific skills.

CAREERS IN THE U.S. MARINE CORPS

ENGINEER, CONSTRUCTION, FACILITIES, AND EQUIPMENT

OccFld 13 includes job designations such as metalworker, engineer equipment mechanic, engineer equipment operator, engineer equipment chief, engineer assistant, combat engineer, and bulk fuel specialist. The men and women working in these specialties deal with all phases of engineering. They maintain, operate, and repair heavy equipment, including bulldozers, cranes, and backhoes; they construct and maintain bridges, offices, residential buildings, warehouses, aircraft hangars, and other needed structures and facilities; and they place and detonate explosive charges for construction and demolition purposes.

TANK AND AMPHIBIOUS ASSAULT VEHICLE

OccFld 18 entails the operation, maneuvering, and maintenance of tracked vehicles in amphibious assaults and the subsequent land operations. A Marine can specialize as a crew member on an Abrams tank, an amphibious assault vehicle (AAV), or an expeditionary fighting vehicle (EFV). Since this field requires its members to serve in combat areas, it is only open to men.

GROUND ORDNANCE MAINTENANCE

Ground Ordnance, OccFld 21, is vital to the success of Marines in combat situations. Marines in this field make sure that everything from small arms to battle tanks is in

AT WORK AS A MARINE

Aircraft Rescue and Firefighting Marines, wearing protective proximity suits, suppress a fire from the propane-fed Mobile Aircraft Firefighting Training Device during a training demonstration.

working order and ready for use. Repair workers and technicians are needed for small arms, towed artillery systems, amphibious assault vehicles, main battle tanks, and light-armored vehicles. Machinists and electro-optical repairmen are two specialties within this field.

CAREERS IN THE U.S. MARINE CORPS

Many Marines have more than one specialty. LCpl. Jonathan M. Griffith works as both an M1A1 main battle tank repair technician and an M1A1 tank crewman.

AMMUNITION AND EXPLOSIVE ORDNANCE DISPOSAL

Marines working in ammunition and explosive ordnance disposal (EOD) (OccFld 23) plan, operate, and manage hazardous material. They are in charge of handling, transporting, and storing the Marine Corps ammunition, explosives, and missiles, and must also inspect these items to determine if any need to be repaired or destroyed. The ammunition technician and EOD technician are the two MOSs in OccFld 23. EOD technicians have a dangerous job: they locate and identify a variety of deadly hazards and then deal with them as necessary to make the location safe.

FOOD SERVICE

OccFld 33 tasks include planning menus, preparing and serving meals, operating and managing the dining facilities, and

AT WORK AS A MARINE

placing orders for food and supplies. Men and women in this field may work at a base or in the field. Formal schooling at Fort Lee, Virginia, is provided and Marines in this OccFld may participate in an apprenticeship program.

MUSIC

Marines who are musically skilled may consider an MOS in OccFld 55–Music. There are several different Marine Corps bands in which an enlisted Marine may play as a musician or serve as a conductor. Instrument repair technicians, drum majors (who lead the ceremonial band when marching), and bandmasters (who evaluate musicians' proficiency and plan and schedule operations and training) are also MOSs in the music field. Additionally, musicians often serve in the field, doubling as security when combat intensity requires it.

METEOROLOGY AND OCEANOGRAPHY

Marines in Meteorology and Oceanography (METOC) (OccFld 68) collect, assess, and disseminate intelligence related to force strengths of other militaries and information (atmospheric, space, climatic, and hydrologic intelligence) necessary in planning and executing operations. Marines attend formal training courses both at the outset of the MOS assignment and throughout their service with METOC, which is the only earth science–related field in the corps. Some specialties include observer, analyst forecaster, and impact analyst.

FIVE

SALARY AND BENEFITS

THERE ARE FINANCIAL, EDUCATIONAL, and personal benefits available to members of the U.S. Marine Corps. The benefits for active-duty enlistees and reservists differ somewhat.

BENEFITS

ENLISTED ACTIVE DUTY

1. Full-time salary
2. Thirty days paid vacation annually
3. Retirement income plus savings program
4. Free medical, dental, and hospital care (includes family members, if married)
5. Low-cost post exchange (PX) (department store) and commissary (grocery store) privileges
6. Low-cost life insurance

Cheryl E. Spencer, the director of the Consolidated Personnel Administration Center, is promoted to Chief Warrant Officer (CWO5) by Lt. Col. William J. Cover (*left*) and Col. Ana R. Smythe (*right*). Spencer is the highest-ranking chief warrant officer at Marine Corps Recruit Depot San Diego.

CAREERS IN THE U.S. MARINE CORPS

7. Extra income includes allowances for subsistence housing and uniforms

RESERVE

1. Part-time salary
2. Full-time pay and allowance for meals and housing during the annual two-week training period
3. Health care for injury or illness during active duty or training periods
4. Low-cost life insurance
5. PX and commissary privileges
6. Retirement program

SALARY AND SPECIAL PAY

Pay for all members of the Marine Corps, enlisted personnel as well as officers, increases with each rank or grade promotion. Salaries also reflect increases in the cost of living allowance (COLA).

EDUCATION

The Marine Corps has always provided its men and women with the facilities and financial means to improve their lives and careers by continuing their education. The Marine Corps, along with the other military branches, offers programs to personnel seeking financial aid and career assistance.

THE MARINE MOTTO AND HYMN

Two of the best-known features of the Marine Corps are its Latin motto—*Semper Fidelis* (always faithful) and its hymn. *Semper Fidelis*, sometimes written as *Semper Fi*, stresses the loyalty and commitment to one's comrades and country that every Marine is expected to show. The phrase has served as the corps' motto since 1883. "Semper Fidelis" is also the title of the corps' official march, which was composed in 1889 by the famed bandleader and composer John Philip Sousa, who was then the director of the U.S. Marine Band. Prior to its adoption, "*Fortitudine*" (with fortitude), "By Sea and by Land," and "From the Halls of Montezuma to the Shores of Tripoli" all served as the corps' motto.

"The Marines' Hymn" is the oldest official song in the U.S. armed forces. Marine recruits are required to memorize at least three stanzas of the hymn. The hymn's opening lines, "From the halls of Montezuma / To the shores of Tripoli," commemorate two major events in which the Marine Corps was involved. The first line refers to U.S. Marines' capture of the National Palace in Mexico City during the Mexican-American War in 1847. The second alludes to the 600-mile (966-km) march through the desert undertaken by the corps in 1805 to attack Tripoli (in North Africa) during the first Barbary War.

CAREERS IN THE U.S. MARINE CORPS

Marines with the special-operations capable 22nd Marine Expeditionary Unit work on math homework during their six-month deployment aboard the USS *Kearsarge*.

THE MONTGOMERY GI BILL AND THE MARINE CORPS COLLEGE FUND

The Montgomery GI Bill (MGIB) and the Marine Corps College Fund (MCCF) are generously endowed government programs that help Marine Corps personnel attain their educational goals.

Marines on active duty, as well as certain members of the Reserve, are eligible to apply for these programs, which are intended to finance a college education. As of 2009, a

SALARY AND BENEFITS

full-time Marine was eligible for approximately $36,000 from the MGIB and up to $50,000 from the MCCF. The money can be used during or after active duty. To qualify, Marines must contribute $100 each month to the Montgomery program for the first twelve months of service. A four-year active-duty contract is required for a new enlistee without any prior service to be eligible for the Marine Corps College Fund.

Reservists who want to take advantage of the Montgomery Bill must enlist for six years and maintain a record of satisfactory drill attendance; they are eligible for up to thirty-six months of educational assistance.

TUITION ASSISTANCE

All active-duty Marines, including selected Marine Corps Reserve members, are eligible for tuition assistance. The military provides up to 100 percent of tuition and educational fees, though there are semester and fiscal year limits to the amount of money a Marine can receive.

Marines can use tuition-assistance funds for vocational-technical, undergraduate, graduate, independent study, and distance-learning programs offered by accredited institutions. Tuition assistance can be used in conjunction with the MGIB.

Marine Corps officers can also receive tuition assistance if they agree to remain on active duty for two years after completing the military-funded course.

CAREERS IN THE U.S. MARINE CORPS

Seventeen-year-old Douglas Cion (*center*), a high school senior from Huntington, New York, received an NROTC scholarship. Cion will participate in the NROTC program at the State University of New York Maritime College and will be commissioned as a second lieutenant in the Marine Corps at graduation. Recruiter Sgt. Marc Plunkett (*left*) and Capt. John Ostman (*right*) stand with Cion.

NROTC SCHOLARSHIPS

The NROTC program offers two-, three-, and four-year scholarships to participating college students that cover tuition and educational fees and include allowances for textbooks and living expenses.

SALARY AND BENEFITS

The scholarship program has strict requirements. Good grades, consistent class attendance, high class ranking, good college entrance examination results, and participation in extracurricular activities are important considerations. After graduation, the newly commissioned officer must fulfill either active-duty or Reserve service.

THE FEW. THE PROUD.

Service in the Marine Corps or the Marine Corps Reserve is admirable and can provide great opportunities and lead to a satisfying career. Information on service in the Army, the Air Force, the Navy, and the Coast Guard is available in the other books in this series, which explain how each branch provides work, adventure, and experience in a wide variety of activities and fields.

ACRONYM GLOSSARY

AAV	Amphibious assault vehicle
ACS	Artillery computer systems
AN/PVS	Army Navy Passive Viewing System
ASVAB	Armed Services Vocational Aptitude Battery
BWT	Basic Warrior Training
COLA	Cost of living allowance
CRRC	Combat rubber reconnaissance craft
CWS	Combat water survival
DEP	Delayed Entry Program
DI	Drill instructor
E	Enlisted, in pay grade designation
EFV	Expeditionary fighting vehicle
EOD	Explosive ordnance disposal
FAST	Fleet Antiterrorism Security Team
HEAA	High-explosive antiarmor
HEDP	High-explosive dual-purpose
IST	Initial strength test
ITB	Infantry Training Battalion
LAV–M	Light-armored vehicle–mortar
MACK	Marine assault climbers kit
MAGTF	Marine Air-Ground Task Force
MARFORRES	Marine Forces Reserve
MBT	Main battle tank
MCB	Marine Corps base
MCCF	Marine Corps College Fund
MCMAP	Marine Corps Martial Arts Program
MCRD	Marine Corps Recruit Depot
MCT Bn	Marine Combat Training Battalion
MEPS	Military Entrance Processing Station
METOC	Meteorology and Oceanography
MEU	Marine Expeditionary Unit

MGIB	Montgomery GI Bill
MOS	Military occupational specialty
NCO	Noncommissioned officer
NROTC	Naval Reserve Officers Training Corps
O	Officer, in pay grade designation
OCC	Officer Candidate Course
OccFld	Occupational field
OCS	Officer Candidate School
PFT	Physical fitness test
PIEK	Parachutist individual equipment kit
PIP	Product improvement program
PLC	Platoon Leader Course
PX	Post exchange; also called base exchange (BX)
RDC	Recruit division commander
ROTC	Reserve Officers Training Corps
RTC	Recruit training command
SAW	Squad automatic weapon
SL/FF RAPS	Static line/Free-fall ram air parachute system
SNCO	Staff noncommissioned officer
SOC	Special Operations Command
TBS	The Basic School
USMCR	United States Marine Corps Reserve
USNA	United States Naval Academy
VTOL	Vertical takeoff/landing
W	Warrant officer, in pay grade designation

FURTHER INFORMATION

WEBSITES

The official website of the U.S. Marine Corps
www.marines.mil

The website of the U.S. Marine Corps Reserve
www.marforres.usmc.mil

The website of the U.S. Marine Corps for new and potential recruits
www.marines.com

The website of the NROTC program
www.nrotc.navy.mil

The website of the U.S. Naval Academy
www.usna.edu

SELECTED BIBLIOGRAPHY

Axelrod, Alan, and Charles Phillips. *Macmillan Dictionary of Military Biography*. New York: Macmillan, 1998.

Chambers, John Whiteclay, II, ed. *Oxford Companion to American Military History*. New York: Oxford University Press, 1999.

Holmes, Richard, ed. *Oxford Companion to Military History*. New York: Oxford University Press, 2001.

Marine Corps Recruit Depot Parris Island. http://www.mcrdpi.usmc.mil (accessed September 8, 2008).

Sturkey, Marion F. *Marine Corps Heritage*. Heritage Press International. http://www.usmcpress.com (accessed September 8, 2008).

INDEX

Page numbers in **boldface** are illustrations, tables, and charts.

active duty, 26, 28–31, 34, 70–71
  enlistee, 71
  officer, 39, 73
Active Duty Special Work (ADSW), 31
Active Reserve (AR) program, 30
aircraft, 20, **21**, 23–25, **57**
Aircraft Rescue and Firefighting, **63**
Air Force Academy, 33
air surveillance radar, **10–11**
Ammunition and Explosive Ordnance Disposal, 64
amphibious assault vehicle (AAV), 62
amphibious raid and reconnaissance equipment, 19–20
antiarmor weapons, 16–18
Armed Services Vocational Aptitude Battery (ASVAB), 42
armor, 18–19
associate duty, 34

Barbary pirates, 8, 22, 69
basic learning phase, 46, 47
Basic Warrior Training (BWT), 49
Belleau Wood, 22
benefits, 11, 66, 68–73
boot camp, 28, **41**, 44–50, **45**, **48**, 61

Camp Lejeune, **7**
Cion, Douglas, **72**
Civil War, 33
Cleaves, David, **13**
combat water survival (CWS), 47
construction career, 62
Continental Marines, 6, 8
core values, 46–49, 55
Cover, William J., **67**
The Crucible, **41**, 49–50

Delayed Entry Program (DEP), **32**, 33, 44
Devil Dogs, 22
drill instructor (DI), 46, **58**, 61

education
  enlistment requirements, 28
  opportunities, 68, 70, **70**, 71
8th Communications Battalion, **7**
engineer career, 62
enlistment, 11, 26, 28, 40–44
  incentives, **7**
  of officer candidates, 54–55
equipment, 12–25
equipment career, 62
Expeditionary Warfare Training Group Pacific, **13**

facilities career, 62
field training phase, 46, 49
fighters aircraft, 20, 22
Fleet Antiterrorism Security Team (FAST), **14**
Food Service career, 64–65

Griffith, Jonathan M., **64**
ground ordnance maintenance, 62–63
Gulf War, 33

Hays, Mary Ludwig, 32–33
helicopters, 20, 23–25, **24**

Individual Mobilization Augmentees (IMA) program, 30
Individual Ready Reserve (IRR), 31, 34
infantry, 58, 60
Infantry Training Battalion (ITB), 50
initial strength test (IST), 28
intelligence, career in, 60

CAREERS IN THE U.S. MARINE CORPS

Iwo Jima Memorial, 50

Jarheads, 22
Jones, Kendall, **29**

Korean War, 33

Lange, Barry, **61**
Lanter, Jesse, **61**
large equipment, 16–20, **17**
LaVine, Lauren, **43**
LaVine, Nicole, **43**
LaVine, Shannon, **43**
Leathernecks, 22
lightweight artillery, 16
Luckett, Mahomad, **45**

machine guns, 15–16, 19, **54**
Marine Combat Training (MCT),
    50, **54**
Marine Corps bands, 65, 69
Marine Corps College Fund, 70, 71
Marine Corps insignia, 50, **52–53**
Marine Corps Martial Arts Program
    (MCMAP), 47
Marine Corps Memorial (Iwo Jima), 50
Marine Corps officers, **53**, 54–55, 71
    salary, 68
    training, 26, 34–39
Marine Corps Recruit Depot (MCRD)
    Parris Island, **32**, 33, 44
    San Diego, 44, **45**, **67**
Marine Expeditionary Forces
    (MEFs), 9
Marine Expeditionary Unit (MEU),
    15, **27**
Marine Forces Reserve
    (MARFORRES), 30, **31**
Marine Air-Ground Task Force
    (MAGTF), **24**

"The Marines' Hymn," 69
McCarthy, Dennis M., **31**
Meteorology and Oceanography
    (METOC) career, 65
midshipmen, 37
Military Academy at West Point, 33
military occupational specialty
    (MOS), 7, 30, 50, 55–56, 74
    identifying designation, **58**
    occupational fields, 56–65, **57**,
        63, **64**
missiles, 19, 20, 23
Mohler, Travis, **10–11**
Montgomery GI Bill (MGIB), 70, 71
motto, 69
music career, 65, 69
MV-22 Osprey, **21**, 25

Naval Reserve Officers Training Corps
    (NROTC), 26, 34–36, **35**, 54
    scholarships, 72–73, **72**
Navy Nurse Corps, 36
Navy Seabees, **59**
nicknames, 22
9th Engineer Support Battalion, **59**

Oath of Enlistment, **7**, 43–44, **43**
occupational fields, 56–65, **57**, **63**, **64**
Officer Candidate Course, 54, 55
Officer Candidate School, **38–39**, 54
on-duty training, 50
Operation Enduring Freedom, **17**
Ostman, John, **72**

pay grades, 51, 55
personnel and administration, 60
physical fitness test, 28, 48, 49
physical standards, 28, 31, 42
physical training, 28, 45–46, 47
Pitcher, Molly, 32

INDEX

Platoon Leaders Class (PLC), 54, 55
Plunkett, Marc, **72**

Ramirez, Felix, **10–11**
ranks, 28, **58**, 68
  of commissioned officers, 55
  enlisted, 51, **52**, 54, 66, 68, 71
  insignia, **52–53**
recruit
  forming, 46
  receiving process, **29**, 46
  training, 46–50
requirements
  for officer training, 54–55
  for NROTC, 36
  for USMC, 26, 28, 40, 42
  for USMCR, 30–31
Reserve Officers Training Corps
  (ROTC), 34, 35
Reserve unit 3rd Battalion, 23rd
  Marine Regiment, **31**
Revolutionary War, 6, 8, 32
Richardson, Tama, **32**, 33
rifle training phase, 46, 47–48

salary, 68–73
scholarships, 36, 72–73, **72**
Selected Marine Corps Reserve
  (SMCR), 30
"Semper Fidelis," 69
Shoemake, Thomas, **27**
small arms, 12, 14, **14**, 15
Smythe, Ana R., **67**
Sousa, John Philip, 69
Spencer, Cheryl E., **67**

tank vehicles, 62
Taras, Ana, **57**
The Basic School (TBS), 55
3rd Battalion, **61**

tour of duty, 28–29, 31, 34, 36, 71
training, **14**, 28
  as career, 61
  matrix, 46
  in MOS, 55, 61
  of officer candidates, 55
  recruit, 46–50
  USMCR, 30
transport aircraft, 20, 23
tuition assistance, 71
22nd Marine Expeditionary Unit, **70**

U.S. Air Force, 23, 25, 28, 34, 46, 73
U.S. Army, 6, 8, 14, 19, 28, 34, 46, 73
U.S. Coast Guard, 73
U.S. Marine Corps Reserve
  (USMCR), 9, 23, 26, 29–31, **31**,
    34, 70–71, 73
U.S. Naval Academy (USNA),
    Annapolis, 26, 33, 37–39, 54
U.S. Navy, 6, 8, 26, 46, 73
USS *Kearsarge*, **70**
USS *Nassau*, **21**

Vietnam War, 9, 33
vocational testing, 42

Wallace, John A., **48**
War on Terrorism, 9
warrant officers, 55, **63**
Washington, George, 6
women, 9, 26, 32–33
  boot camp, 44
  in NROTC, 35–36
  prohibited areas, 33, 58, 62
  in USNA, 37
Women's Armed Services
    Integration Act, 33
World War I, 22, 33
World War II, 22, 33

ABOUT THE AUTHOR

EDWARD F. DOLAN is the author of more than 120 published nonfiction books. His most recent book for Marshall Cavendish Benchmark is *George Washington* in the series Presidents and Their Times. Mr. Dolan is a California native and currently resides near San Francisco.